D0597874

LOFTS

ROCKPORT

LOFTS

NEW DESIGNS FOR URBAN LIVING   Felicia Eisenberg Molnar

GLOUCESTER MASSACHUSETTS

ROCKPORT PUBLISHERS

Copyright © 2001 by Rockport Publishers, Inc.

All rights reserved. No part of this book may be
reproduced in any form without written permission
of the copyright owners. All images in this book
have been reproduced with the knowledge and prior
consent of the artists concerned and no responsibility
is accepted by producer, publisher, or printer for any
infringement of copyright or otherwise, arising from
the contents of this publication. Every effort has
been made to ensure that credits accurately comply
with information supplied.

First published in the United States of America by
Rockport Publishers, Inc.
33 Commercial Street
Gloucester, Massachusetts 01930-5089
Telephone: (978) 282-9590
Facsimile: (978) 283-2742
www.rockpub.com

ISBN 1-56496-777-8

10 9 8 7 6 5

Designer: Leeann Leftwich

Cover image:

      Rosenberg Residence and Studio by
      Belmont Freeman Architects.
      photo: Christopher Wesnofske.

Back cover images:

      (top) Tribeca Loft by
      Tow Studios.
      photo: Bjorg Arnarsdottir.

      (bottom) Bay Loft by
      Brayton Hughes Design Studio.
      photo: John Sutton.

Printed in China.

To Imre and Isabelle and the building of dreams.

CONTENTS

PREFACE

The birth of residential loft living is often dated to the late 1950s in the SoHo district of Manhattan. Affordable studio and living space for creative young urbanites was hard to find. Artists and craftspeople turned to abandoned factory buildings, whose generous scale offered relatively cheap, and often illegal, working-living studios. As the city fathers began to see the benefits of this reconversion, laws were adjusted to encourage redevelopment and soon, artists were joined by young professionals seeking an alternative to conventional city apartments. Trendy cafés, restaurants, and galleries took root and real estate values soared in these once-forgotten neighborhoods.

The appeal of loft living is instantly apparent. Lofts are romantic places. Banks of windows and towering ceilings speak of unusual heights, intense luminosity, open spaces, and personal freedom in cramped city environments. A loft offers a tabula rasa where the urban dweller can cast a wide net in seemingly endless space.

While lofts are full of exciting possibilities, knowing how to live in a loft and tackle the task of transformation may seem daunting. What to do with the lack of walls or hallways? What about sprinkler systems, windows that have no view or let in too much light, concrete floors stained with paint, and rumbling air conditioning and heating ducts overhead? How to handle open space that has not been delineated into bedroom, bath, and kitchen? To the untrained eye, crushed under the soaring magnitude of a former powerhouse or ice cream factory, a loft's almost inconceivable immensity may seem uninhabitable.

By understanding the options, however, one can start to savor the bigness and distinguish the openness. The impersonality vanishes and the dreaming can begin. Converting a leather tannery or former printing plant into a place to call home takes creativity and imagination.

This book is concerned with the unfolding of that dream. It offers inspiration—that clean contemporary lines really can float above an aging landscape. Offering a peek at how architects, interior designers and loft dwellers can weave a barren, formerly industrial space into a home—in the most wonderful sense of the word—is its mission.

This project grows out of many years spent peering into lofts in the cities around the world, at all times of the day and night, dreaming dreams of designing, living, and working in a loft. At some stage, savoring lofts and drinking them in visually is not enough; one wants to find out not just who designed them but who lives in them and what they do.

Loft dwellers seem to be the most fascinating of all urban dwellers. They are the heroes of our modern cities who have fought to rescue and preserve the city without destroying it, turning grand monuments of the past into grand residences of the future. Once-forgotten neighborhoods in many cities have been restored to some of the most exciting residences on the planet.

Today, New York's artists, designers, and other loft residents largely still hold the cutting edge in loft design. While the supply of building stock is diminishing, the original pioneering spirit to discover even more neglected neighborhoods in cities around the world continues. This book offers a rare glimpse at New York's influence, both subtle and obvious, on loft design internationally.

LOFT SPACE THE NEW URBAN DWELLING

by George Ranalli

There is much in loft design to theorize about. Issues such as family organization, multiple families in relation to each other, and the community of families at the scale of the city are open for investigation. In loft design, domestic arrangements are not predetermined. All levels of public and private human interaction are open for interpretation. Design for loft living is giving shape to new ideas about domestic life, which are in turn providing a substantive transformation in traditional residential design around the world.

Loft living has been primarily an American phenomenon but is becoming a sought-after dwelling type for urbanites in many cities around the world. Most often, neglected and rediscovered building stock offers spaces that are long and narrow, with windows either on two ends or along one long wall. Whatever the configuration, the found condition usually presents a strong beginning and, generally, a visible, bare-bones structure.

The challenge in working with loft space is to provide the necessary residential—and sometimes work—amenities, without sacrificing the open, light, and free-flowing quality of the original space. Each loft presents a new, different, and challenging spatial problem. Existing windows, elevators, and stairs are strong determinants to the organization of the loft design. These predetermined elements often give a puzzlelike quality to the problem at hand. The goal is ultimately to fulfill all the necessary light and space requirements and still create a compelling, functional design that preserves a relationship to the original building.

LEFT Axonometric drawing of the K-Loft designed by George Ranalli. The project was a 2,100-square-foot (195.1-square-meter) loft that integrated original brick walls of the former industrial building with a series of new forms and custom decorative objects.

The archaeology of a loft space is often materially rich and somewhat rough in finish. As most lofts were once industrial spaces, the unfinished masonry provides a striking texture to the environment and provides designers and inhabitants with rooms of strong character and history.

In my own work on lofts, I always endeavor to explore the needs of public and personal family life to yield the possibility of new, untried domestic arrangements. We take for granted that the public realm is for family and group rituals while the private spaces of domestic life should allow individuals to dwell in their thoughts, feelings, and dreams. The specific alterations and interpretations of a wide-open loft space can produce some interesting spatial and familial arrangements and relationships that are not readily accommodated in conventional residential architecture. For example, the Peter Anders loft on page 118 was a study in new ways of living for two families sharing a single loft space. This necessitated novel solutions including common areas and connecting elements to bridge the private areas.

The exploration of materials and forms is also very dynamic in loft design. An intimate dialogue of these two elements can be experimented with in unusual ways. Detail, too, is the last and ultimately most important component of loft projects. Details reflect the complex technical and aesthetic idea and contribute to the overt beauty of the design, specifically through their form and proportion.

The seamless relationship of a new design for loft living to the existing condition of the building as a historical artifact is, finally, paramount. The search must always be for a coherent, clear, and sometimes innovative idea about domestic life that can be expressed in material beauty. This is the challenge of loft design that is highlighted in many of the projects featured on the pages that follow.

George Ranalli is professor of architectural design at Yale University, and maintains a private architecture practice in New York City. Mr. Ranalli's work has been exhibited internationally and is part of the permanent collection of twentieth century art and design at the Metropolitan Museum of Art. He has been the subject of two monographs, and his work has been published widely around the world.

ABOVE Newport Residence, conversion of a National Register Historic Landmark schoolhouse into six loft units. The spaces are fronted with an interior façade behind which the smaller, more private rooms are arranged.

LOFT DESIGN IN NEW YORK CITY

With its vibrant, gutsy, imaginative culture, New York evokes envy in the world at large. In the 1950s, Manhattan's dreamers and visionaries gave the modern age an inspiring model for converting redundant industrial buildings and creating space for a new class of urban dwellers. This trend, started largely by artists and craftspeople, was both innovative and illegal at first. The city fathers eventually realized that a terrific opportunity existed for redevelopment and rewrote the law books to encourage conversion of these formerly commercial zones. In designs for loft living, New York City holds the world's attention.

Today, abandoned buildings in neglected neighborhoods of Manhattan still signal a nirvana of wide-open space with exciting opportunities for creative self-expression and grand-scale living. In the New York vision of loft living, traditional forms are analyzed and reconfigured. The industrial-to-domestic transformation is organic, growing out of the surrounding environment. A former fur factory, bank building, or food warehouse forms a perfect beginning. Cast-off trusses and other industrial parts may be reassembled in nonstandard

ways. Geometries are sometimes created that organize the industrial members through the structure. Often concrete or steel girders, airflow ducts, or freight elevators remain as testimony to the history of the space. Their beauty and usefulness elicits a sense of contact with the building's original character.

Minimalism and functionality determined many interiors of New York's first living and working lofts. In this age of less is more, when excess is becoming a thing of the past, the focus remains on minimalism. However, the rich variety of materials and fine craftsmanship exhibited in the following pages refutes the argument that Gotham City design is cold, slick, and untouchable. Glass and steel can gleam with jewel-like precision, wood reveals its sensual texture, and concrete can seem warm. These qualities found in many New York lofts continue to inspire Europeans and others. Design Manhattan-style teaches that loft living can be generous even when space is at a premium. In the designing of lofts, New Yorkers aspire to a kind of personal utopia that nurtures their individual visions—a trend that the world, it seems, wants to follow and build on.

Urban Interface Loft
DEAN/WOLF ARCHITECTS

AFTER LIVING IN a series of city apartments where natural light was a rare presence, the owners-designers sought a home where the city meets the sky. Within the overbuilt skyline of Manhattan, this dream was not so easy to realize. After a long search, the couple and a group of friends adopted an entire six-story, dilapidated electrical warehouse in Tribeca. An intricate financial partnership was born to finance the project; Kathryn Dean and Charles Wolf agreed to serve as the architects of record for the building-wide renovation in exchange for taking the most valuable top-floor space. While their own loft is small, the design is grand, with the focus on the skies above. The key design element is a courtyard carved out of the roof. Light and views are drawn into the space through clerestories and light scoops. Inside, a sandblasted-glass partition divides the work studio from the living areas. Copper sheeting meets other materials in a carefully considered order.

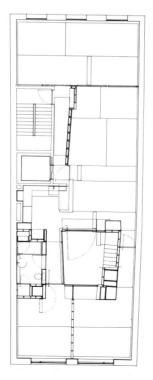

ABOVE The loft is focused on the skies above with a courtyard cut out of the roof.

LEFT Top-floor plan.

OPPOSITE At twilight the city recedes and the loft comes into focus.

ABOVE View of central stairway to roof.

LEFT Axonometric diagram showing the new courtyard, clerestories, and light scoops inserted into the existing structure.

OPPOSITE Juxtaposed materials reflect light in a view down the central axis of the loft.

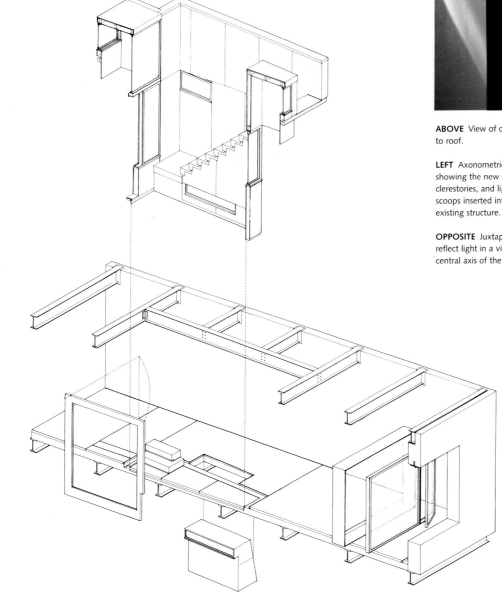

The Ultimate Loft

MOST LOFT DWELLERS seem to prefer minimalist interiors devoid of any resemblance to the urban chaos lurking outside. Not the architect Malcolm Holzman and his wife Andrea Landsman. They filled their Manhattan loft with fanciful remnants from the world of stuff, referring to their collection joyfully as junk. "For our loft, I did what my clients won't let me do," says Holzman. Aside from the couple's distinguished collection of American realist paintings and contemporary sculpture, the loft is a study in playful eccentricity. The architect paid close attention to unusual materials and finishes. Some walls are covered with galvanized steel stamped in alternating brick and stone patterns. Other materials would be more commonly found in gas stations, highway strip buildings, or industrial shacks—including green-stained flakeboard and corrugated fiberglass. Overall, however, the composition and color choices are extraordinarily skillful. The loft is a testing ground for new ideas—experiments for which some may not be ready.

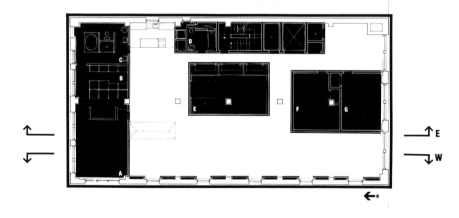

ABOVE View out of the loft. Anthropomorphic lamp is by Harry Anderson.

LEFT Floor plan.

OPPOSITE Materials and colors collide in the spacious living area.

ABOVE Galvanized, stamped steel in alternating brick and stone patterns on the wall. Dining table consists of slabs of Georgia marble.

OPPOSITE A Blatz Beer sign ornaments the kitchen. The plates are gifts from friends and are accepted by the owners only if they cost less than one U.S. dollar.

RIGHT A view toward the kitchen and adjacent walls of transluscent fiberglass, with original concrete beams and columns.

34th Street Loft
LOT/EK ARCHITECTURE

LOT/EK HAS BROUGHT new meaning to the term "found objects." In this renovated loft, Guisseppe Lugnano and Ada Tolla have performed a masterful feat of architectural wizardry. As designers, they were interested in maintaining the inherent beauty and character of the 2,000-square-foot (185.8-square-meter) loft situated in Manhattan's Garment District. The client's desire for openness and the need for privacy were not easy to achieve in sleeping, cooking, and bathing areas. To resolve this, LOT/EK brought in the 40-foot (12.2-meter) side of an aluminum shipping container to serve as the major space organizer. The metal plane slices through the space to separate domestic areas from the clients' work studio. To provide flexibility and access, a series of incisions was made to create hinged or pivoting panels. Three full-height panels pivot to reveal the bedroom, while smaller hinged panels allow access to kitchen equipment. This aluminum "partition" terminates in the bathroom, where it divides the shower and toilet from an anteroom wash area.

BATHROOM

KITCHEN

BEDROOM

LIVING/STUDIO

mobile work station

multi-functional wall

ABOVE AND OPPOSITE Panels in an aluminum plane, which runs the length of the loft, conceal kitchen equipment; the panel above the stove opens up, like a garage door. When closed, only the sink, oven and shipping container graphics are revealed.

LEFT Floor plan.

ABOVE Hinged panel doors cut into the aluminum plane pivot to open up the bedroom to the main space. A television, set into a panel door, is visible in the bedroom when the panels are open and from the larger living area when the doors pivot shut.

RIGHT Recycled refrigerators provide both storage and work surface for the artist couple who occupy this 2,000-square-foot (185.8-square-meter) loft space. Set perpendicular to the aluminum metal plane, a pipe carries bundled electrical cords to provide lighting and power to the work stations.

OPPOSITE The aluminum plane runs the length of the loft, concealing the kitchen, bedroom, and bath from working areas. Existing concrete floors were polished.

Quandt Loft

TOD WILLIAMS, BILLIE TSIEN AND ASSOCIATES

COOL, STRICT, INFORMAL elegance characterize this impeccably balanced 5,000-square-foot (464.5-square-meter) loft in New York City's Greenwich Village. Designed by the award-winning husband-and-wife team Tod Williams and Billie Tsien, the loft embodies harmony, equilibrium and a sense of tension among its elements. Generous flowing space is retained through the use of sliding doors and walls—hung from the ceiling—that move, closing off or opening up various spaces around the main living area. Despite its size, the loft's plan is simple, with a central, terrazzo-floored living space encircled by more private areas. A long wall of windows allows natural light to enter, while the varying hues of the pigmented-plaster, from mauve to beige, also create a sense of light and movement. The architects, working in close collaboration with artists, metal fabricators, and cabinetmakers, paid close attention to all aspects of construction.

ABOVE A translucent wall telescopes on tracks to open the bathroom to the master bedroom.

LEFT Floor plan.

OPPOSITE Views of the main living space with black plywood bookcases floating in the center.

ABOVE Sleeping and living areas are separated by a sliding wall suspended from an overhead track.

OPPOSITE A cantilevered arm holding a handblown glass flower vase is featured in the entry foyer.

Family Living Loft

SCOTT MARBLE · KAREN FAIRBANKS ARCHITECTS

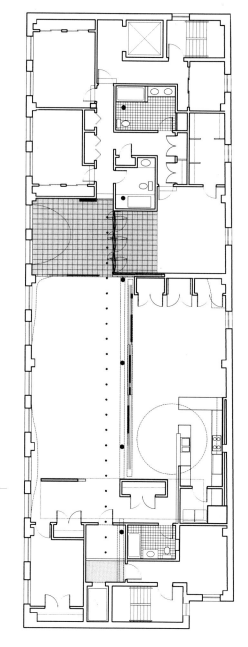

FLEXIBLE LIVING SPACE for a family of four in a crowded urban environment is not easy to achieve. In this 4,500-square-foot (418.1-square-meter) conversion of an industrial building in the Chelsea neighborhood of New York City, the designers have created a nontraditional domestic organization for a two-bedroom, two-bathroom family loft. A variety of transformative elements has been devised to negotiate the demands of privacy with the desire for open space. A series of four sliding wood and glass panels and three pivoting doors are the organizing structures that divide the loft into formal and informal spaces. In this otherwise minimalist environment, geometric shapes across the panels and doors are given definition with rich materials including aluminum, wood, and etched glass. The ability of the loft to adjust to multiple domestic activities was given high priority by the husband-and-wife design team.

LEFT Loft floor plan.

OPPOSITE View from the entry. Sliding panels at right separate formal dining and living areas from informal kitchen and family zones. At the far end, the sliding panel that divides the formal living area from the study is open.

ABOVE View of pivoting doors from the study toward parents' bedroom.

OPPOSITE From within the bedroom cork flooring stained dark lends contrast to maple floors elsewhere.

ABOVE View of living area with sliding panel between living area and study in place.

OPPOSITE View of all three sliding panels fully extended between formal and informal living areas.

Tribeca Loft
TOW STUDIOS

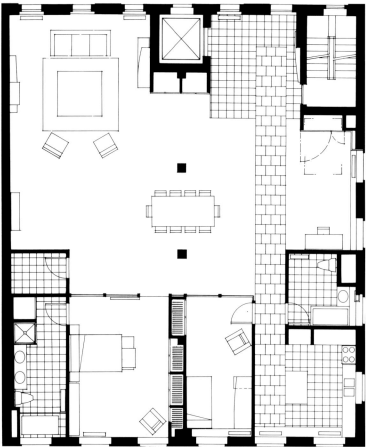

LOCATED IN THE heart of a bustling New York City nightclub area, this 2,800-square-foot (260.1-square-meter) loft occupies an entire floor of a recently converted building. The space was stripped bare to the concrete beams, floors, and masonry walls to make way for a simple, peaceful, wide-open, two-bedroom, two-bathroom living space. Windows line three walls of the building and the elevator opens directly into the loft. Translucent glass doors and walls were constructed to allow natural light to flow deep into the center and beyond to the darker areas. The architect mixed maple with flame-finished French limestone slabs to create a kind of trail within the flooring. This pathway connects the entry on the west to the kitchen on the east. A frosted-glass wall with a sliding glass panel runs north-south, screening the bedrooms from the dining area. The screen glows when the morning sun fills the bedrooms or when the lights are turned on in the evening.

ABOVE Loft floor plan.

RIGHT Elevator entry features stuccoed wall finished in traditional Italian style, adding pigments to the final coat of the plaster and sanding and polishing the surface.

OPPOSITE Dining room with view out to kitchen area, showing limestone "path" and maple floor.

ABOVE The spacious, wide-open main living area.

ABOVE Bedrooms and kitchen are situated along perimeter walls to allow for maximum interior living area.

Renaud Loft
CHA & INNERHOFFER ARCHITECTURE + DESIGN

MODERNIST THEMES OF plane and volume, opacity and transparency, juxtaposed with classical elements are explored in the Renaud Loft. The original 4,000 square feet (371.6 square meters) of space in a converted five-story, landmark building were adapted for the private residence of a young banker. Designed to serve as a quiet refuge from chaotic urban life, the loft provides an elegant setting for entertaining and accommodating frequent guests. The design team divided the loft along two very fluid lines for private and public functions. This movement and interplay of functions is delineated by the sensual interaction of materials such as cherry, walnut, limestone, and frosted glass. The introduction of various moving planes, such as sliding and pivoting doors, further enriches the perception of light, space, and texture between the two functional areas of the loft.

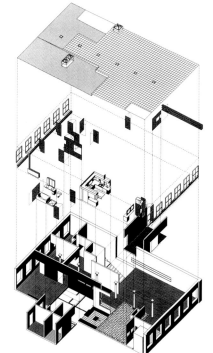

ABOVE AND OPPOSITE
Classical columns—an original feature of this former department store, now a registered landmark building—offer a counterpoint to inserted modernist planes of cherry, walnut, and frosted glass.

LEFT Exploded axonometric.

ABOVE Walnut and frosted glass create plane and volume in this otherwise minimal loft space. The white vinyl couch and chair provide stark elegance within a contemporary architectural envelope.

OPPOSITE The manipulation of materials, details, and finishes is most evident in the kitchen. French limestone floors, cherry cabinetry, and stainless steel elegantly transform an other-wise purely functional room.

Fifth Avenue Loft

SCOTT MARBLE · KAREN FAIRBANKS ARCHITECTS

USING TRANSPARENT, TRANSLUCENT, and opaque materials, this lower-Fifth Avenue loft makes great use of a tight space and minimal natural light. Commissioned by a choreographer, the 1,400-square-foot (130-square-meter) renovation includes two bedrooms and bathrooms that were organized along a series of dynamic planes running longitudinally from the entry to the window wall. These planes range from glass rods and various types of plate glass to sliding veneered plywood and glass panels that are designed to accommodate private and public living. The guest room is adjacent to the kitchen and can become a dining area by opening the sliding panels or can become privately linked to the bathroom by closing the cherry panels. A range of furnishings from the modern era give warmth to an otherwise predominantly industrial space.

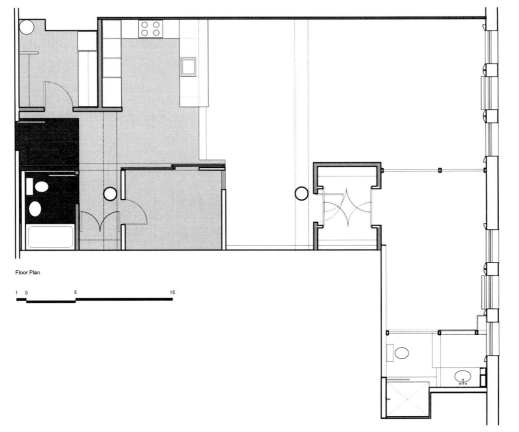

Floor Plan

1 0   5   15

LEFT Floor plan.

OPPOSITE Three panels of windows are one of only two sources of natural light in this relatively small downtown loft.

ABOVE Translucent panels provide a sense of light and brightness in the bedroom.

OPPOSITE Sliding panels to the left allow the guest room to be transformed into a formal dining area for entertaining.

Divney Residence
HUT SACHS STUDIO

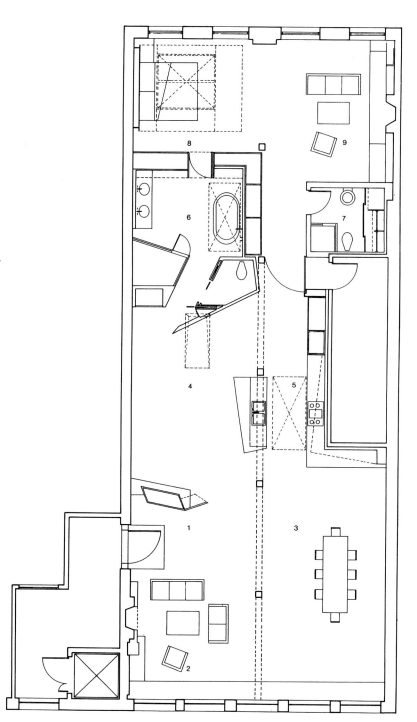

DEDICATED TO RESTORATION and renovation, the handlers of the downtown Divney residence clearly cherished it as an historic place. The client's affection for craftsmanship is further echoed in the fine detailing of this 2,300-square-foot (213.7-square-meter) residence. Salvaged brick has been reconfigured into a fireplace for the living room, where original wood beams and columns have been left exposed. Cherry cabinetry and gold leaf are used extensively throughout the space, along with custom tiles and other hand-sculpted wood detailing. The architects have reconciled the rawness of an old commercial building with the refined forms of the new construction, allowing each to maintain its identity.

LEFT Floor plan.

OPPOSITE Cozy living area features a fireplace crafted from salvaged bricks.

ABOVE Master bedroom features skylight and wood planes, limiting the need for decorative objects.

LEFT The client's affection for handcraftsmanship is in evidence throughout the details of the loft.

OPPOSITE Exposed heavy timber beams, new cherry cabinetry, and maple flooring are bathed in daylight from large overhead skylights.

Hudson Loft

ALEXANDER GORLIN ARCHITECT

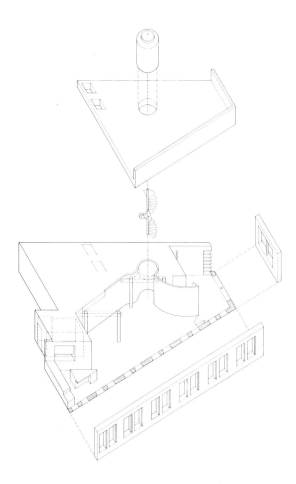

MATERIALS THAT SEEM more expensive than they are and odd floor plan feature predominantly in this loft commissioned by a young family. Stainless-steel counters were installed at half the cost of stone. Cabinets that appear to be faced in ebonized wood are really laminated. A sinuous wall of concave and convex curves extends the length of the loft, which is triangular in plan. The main living area is anchored on one end by a postindustrial kitchen with west-facing windows. The center island was designed to replicate the footprint of the building. On the far end of the living room, a spiral staircase is set within a curving wall ascending to the rooftop garden. The loft's plan culminates in the master bathroom, located on the other side of the spiral staircase. The grottolike tub and shower are sculpted out of the curve of the staircase wall and covered in cobalt blue tile.

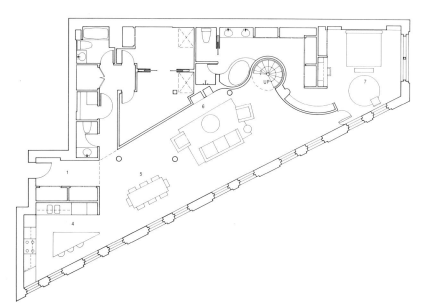

ABOVE Exploded axonometric.

LEFT Floor plan.

OPPOSITE Sinuous curving walls in the living area act as bookcases and play against a spiral staircase to the rooftop garden.

ABOVE Master bath is tucked behind a compound curve that forms part of the living room wall.

RIGHT The postindustrial kitchen features stainless-steel cabinetry that reflects light from the west-facing windows.

Wei Loft
BAK ARCHITECTURE

LIGHT FEATURES MOST strongly in this tranquil New York City loft. Both luxuriantly sensuous and utterly modest, the design is committed to accommodating everyday life with its constant adaptions and nuanced perceptions. Birch walls and textile screens have been placed into the preexisting volume to suggest spatial displacement and light sources lying beyond the apparent perimeter of a given enclosure. The designers collaborated brilliantly here in creating an idiosyncratic layout of basic rooms and in the ingenious accommodation of objects owned by the client. This creativity is most evident in the library, where two free-standing bookcases have been deftly incorporated into the built-in book-storage walls. Translucent panels, faced in canvas, appear on three separate occasions. These fixed and sliding screens act to create privacy, and to enliven and filter light throughout the space.

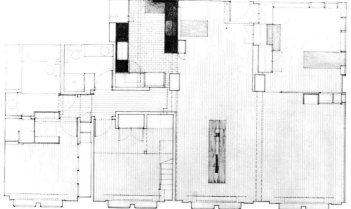

ABOVE View from kitchen includes translucent panels and new cabinets.

LEFT Floor plan.

OPPOSITE View of the entry and library. Order and privacy have been created by custom-designed, birch-inlaid walls and translucent screens.

ABOVE The master bedroom is filled with natural light.

OPPOSITE ABOVE Flowing space links kitchen to living area.

OPPOSITE BELOW Partial plan and perspective view.

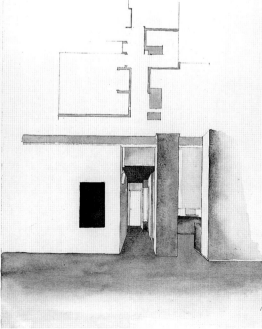

City Loft
VICENTE WOLF ASSOCIATES, INC.

FURNITURE AND ART objects originating from countries as far and wide as France, Sweden, China, and Thailand in this loft make a very personal statement of the owner-designer's most intimate tastes and love of travel. Neutral tones and simple, spare interior space feature predominately in the design. Balance is achieved with a variety of scales and the use of freestanding objects. An eclectic blend of black and white furniture and photographs is woven together with concrete floors painted white. Stone, linen, and leather in neutral tones lend a variety of textures to the loft. Artwork is rarely hung on the walls but placed at important locations to capture and focus attention. The surrounding cityscape becomes a feature of the space—the owner-designer chose to eliminate window treatments.

ABOVE Desk and stool are some of the freestanding pieces that add to a variety of scales in the loft.

OPPOSITE Living area features neutral furniture, painted walls, and a concrete floor painted white.

OPPOSITE Furniture and objects from around the globe reflect the owner-designer's love of travel.

RIGHT AND BELOW White is dominant in this bedroom, which is accented with black and white photographs.

Chelsea Loft
KAR HO ARCHITECT

THIS 1,200-SQUARE-FOOT (111.5-square-meter) Chelsea loft is a showcase for the owner-designer's collection of brightly colored furnishings and decorative objects dating from the 1960s. Finished in white paint, the loft was first stripped down to wood floors and perimeter walls. With ceilings stretching to 9 feet (2.7 meters), the biggest challenge for the architect was to bring natural light into the space from one large window on the north side of the building. To maximize the sensation of light and create spatial depth, frosted-glass screens and doors were designed. As the client lives alone, the need to create privacy with walls was unnecessary. In the bathroom, which is very long and without sunlight, frosted glass was again employed to create the illusion of natural light.

ABOVE Frosted-glass entry door brings indirect light into the kitchen.

OPPOSITE A feeling of spaciousness is achieved in this small loft through limited dividing walls and fresh white paint.

ABOVE As the owner lives alone, the architect was free to create an open plan.

LEFT Frosted-glass mirrors in the bathroom create the sensation of windows in a long, narrow room otherwise lacking in natural light.

OPPOSITE Brightly colored objects are set off against the neutral tones and large volume of the loft.

RIGHT Sitting room painted white provides a serene backdrop for the owner's collection of 1960s furnishings.

Rosenberg Residence and Studio
BELMONT FREEMAN ARCHITECTS

THE DIVISION OF work space at home is often difficult to achieve. In this project, the owner was in the enviable situation of having two spaces stacked vertically, one on top of the other. In renovating this pair of 1,500-square-foot (139.4-square-meter) floors, the architects both emphasized the vertical separation and developed a material language to unite them.

With impressive views of the city beyond, the interior space is quiet and serene. The architects accented the connection between the living and working floors not with a conventional staircase but with a ship's ladder pitched at 75 degrees, which presents a challenging climb. Lighting further creates a distinction between the two levels. The studio features businesslike track lighting and a group of pendant lamps by William Lescaze. The main residence features a mix of standing and table lamps, with indirect halogen lamps illuminating the long, white kitchen wall.

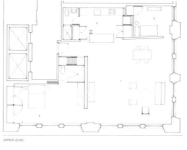

UPPER LEVEL

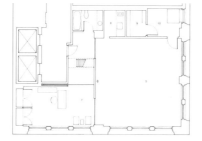

ABOVE A view of the building from the Manhattan street shows the two levels illuminated at dusk.

LEFT Floor plans, living area above and studio below.

OPPOSITE A ship's ladder connects the two levels while providing a significant transition between work and living areas. Cold-rolled steel doors have been finished with automotive wax.

LEFT The upper level includes the living room, kitchen and two bedrooms. The owner's collection of mid-century modernist furniture is featured throughout.

BELOW On the lower studio level, the original concrete floors have been refinished, as have the radiators, which were removed, sandblasted, and sprayed with molten zinc.

ABOVE The stainless-steel kitchen is accented by a floating maple countertop box with drawers. The original concrete floor has been refinished.

RIGHT The washroom becomes the lobby area for the concealed shower/wet room. This room features a 2-in-thick (5-cm-thick) cedar ceiling to contain moisture. The stainless-steel sink is cantilevered on steel braces.

Live/Work Dualities Loft
DEAN/WOLF ARCHITECTS

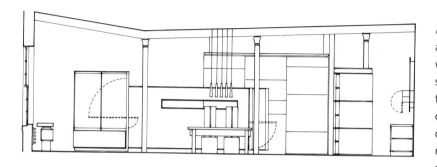

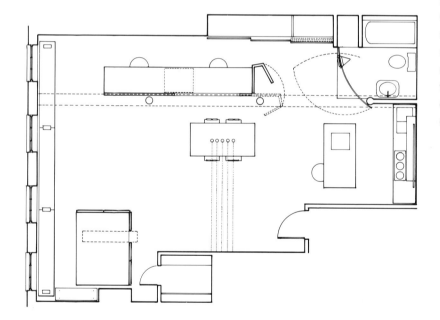

A TOP-FLOOR space filled with light was the most appealing original feature of this small Tribeca loft, which was adapted for living and working in the same space. The design strategy for the 875 square feet (81.3 square meters) of open space was to create an "operable collage" system of movable components. Visual connections expand both real and perceived dimensions among three primary spaces that include workroom, bedroom, and bathroom.

The shell of the loft space was left intact with cast-iron columns, wood floors, and plaster walls that were refurbished and painted. Constructed elements were positioned against this neutral ground. Concrete, steel, and heavy timber are the structural elements making up each piece. Juxtaposed with these rugged materials are delicate fabric infills—canvas, cotton, wool, and woven aluminum—that enhance a wonderful air of domesticity.

ABOVE Section and floor plan.

OPPOSITE Detail view of workroom wall and aperture. Juxtaposed materials enhance light reflection. A birch-plywood and woven-aluminum screen isolates the sleeping quarters from the kitchen/dining area.

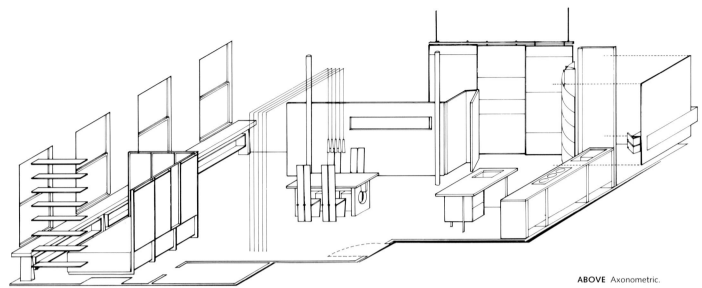

ABOVE Axonometric.

BELOW LEFT View of steel and canvas screen.

BELOW RIGHT Canvas and steel bathroom door in foreground with view to living area.

ABOVE LEFT AND RIGHT
Cherry and steel chairs in the
dining room, with the
workroom wall and translucent
screen beyond.

Artist's Studio

GALIA SOLOMONOFF PROJECTS

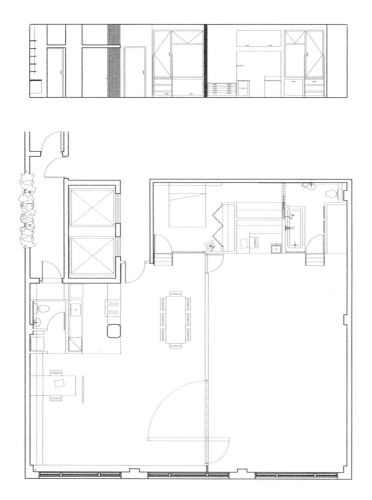

LOCATED IN A former fur factory dating to 1910, this loft in its found condition featured a broken freight elevator, an unusable bathroom, and a precarious old pantry in the kitchen. The building is a reinforced concrete structure with massively oversized beams and columns. Working on a very tight budget, the owner-designer converted this 2,000-square-foot (185.8-square-meter) loft into a residence in less than ten weeks. The designer's husband, an artist, had one firm request: He wanted to be able to look at his paintings in the studio from a blue bathtub. Following their own fantasies, the couple divided the 48-by-44-foot (14.6-by-13.4-meter) space in half, between the studio and living space. The loft makes the best of work and domestic life possible with the north wall featuring a raised platform to accommodate the master bed, bath, and other private elements while offering a generous working area. Off-the-shelf industrial materials including glass, aluminum, and other standard commercial items seldom used for residential interiors are central to the character of this well-designed loft.

ABOVE Floor plan.

OPPOSITE A dividing wire-mesh panel in the library is hung from the ceiling slab using steel rods. Original windows feature a bench flanking the radiators, screened under wire mesh.

ABOVE Beyond the dining area a stepladder leads to a raised sleeping platform, which can be closed off for privacy, with bathroom and walk-in closet.

OPPOSITE Domestic functions of kitchen-laundry-pantry are efficiently packed under a light aluminum canopy in an area that was formerly the elevator shaft. The refrigerator and stove were found in a second-hand restaurant supply shop in the Bowery.

Tribeca Home and Studio
MONEO BROCK ARCHITECTS

THIS DOWNTOWN LOFT is found on the top floor of a ten-floor warehouse that dates back to 1898. To assure a feeling of spaciousness, the designers cut open the roof at strategic locations and installed skylights or large clerestory windows. The glass in the main living area provides light deep into the space and also provides exciting views of the building's rooftop water tank. A folding aluminum ship's ladder serves as the access to the rooftop garden. The ladder was designed with a landing made of glass tiles and is rigged to a counterweight that can easily be lifted overhead to clear the way for additional working space. The warehouse's original columns and beams were left intact in select locations around the loft to promote the feeling of stout solidity. A custom-designed cabinet with translucent glass divides the working area from living space.

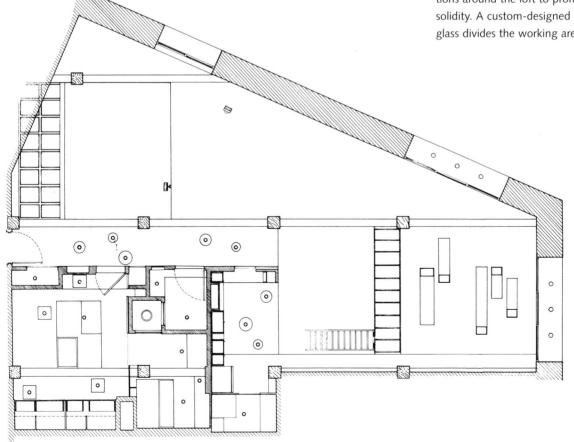

LEFT Floor plan.

OPPOSITE View from the work area through the loft to skylit ship's ladder. Pressboard wall provides privacy for kitchen.

OPPOSITE FAR RIGHT Above the dining area, a majestic clerestory wall opens onto the rooftop and water tower.

ABOVE Frosted-glass landing bridge allows a close-up look out to the cityscape and skies above.

ABOVE RIGHT The romantic rooftop garden sits under the water tower.

ABOVE LEFT Kitchen area is small but functional, with carefully designed cabinetry.

ABOVE Working studio features high ceilings, large clerestories, and plenty of natural light.

GOING GLOBAL

In a world of shrinking resources, the revitalization of redundant buildings is becoming a priority around the globe. Disillusionment with current construction has led many to build a new order within preexisting conventions. Lofts are a perfect repository for these aspirations. In London, members of the trendy set have been converting buildings in former commercial dockyards. In Tokyo, where space has always been at a premium, loft developments are growing out of nondescript and unassuming warehouse buildings. With newly prosperous commercial cities requiring even newer facilities, city governments are seeing an advantage in promoting the conversion of former libraries or exchange buildings into residential loft developments.

To some a loft is nothing more than a concrete shell with unfinished floors and walls. But an open space seemingly bereft of warmth offers those with a creative eye the chance to express themselves. While stereotypes may dictate that a loft is only a loft if it is furnished with black leather, stainless steel, and a few black-and-white photographs, loft living is really about stripping away all preconceived notions. When it comes to interior planning and arranging furniture, knowing where to start is not easy, but comfort should be paramount.

One of the key challenges of loft design is the integration of a building's past and present. To achieve this union, lofts worldwide are often like tapestries—woven elements of contradictory associations. Often alluded to is the modernist quest for rational design and order. But in seeking to go beyond a raw industrial look, lofts often defy expectations, offering a compromise between traditional fragments and pure, open space. Function and fantasy often share the same space, nurturing a sense of personal utopia. With designers and architects pushing clients to the limits of materials and expression, loft design can also be driven by the wish for stability and security.

What is most remarkable about designs for loft living around the world is that they often seem to defy local cultural formalities. Loft living implicitly recognizes individuals and our desire to create meaning apart from the social world. Thus, a loft is perhaps the truest residence for the global village and world citizens. Resisting the temptations of trends and tradition, the lofts that follow offer a contemporary way of living in a wide variety of cultural landscapes across the globe.

Carlson-Reges Residence
RoTo ARCHITECTS, INC.

THE CULT OF the individual in the city of Los Angeles often translates into maverick architectural projects. Partners Michael Rotondi and Clark Stevens of the Los Angeles–based RoTo Architects remodeled the machine shop of the city's first electrical power station in a former industrial belt near downtown. A compelling architectural vision transformed the building into a loft of unusual character.

While retaining the structure's raw, open nature, the building was metamorphosed into a state of unpredictable comfort. The architects blurred the boundaries of spatial divisions with a geometry that jumps back and forth between old and new, inside and outside, up and down. Concrete and steel are juxtaposed with redwood decks and a lush rain-forest garden. Windows and door frames were removed to allow pieces of new steel armature to penetrate open expanses in the original pavilion enclosure. Interior and exterior spaces flow inside and out.

ABOVE The exterior was reconfigured and a steel shell was added atop the existing concrete and steel pavilion, which contains the bedroom annex. Angular steel panels support rooftop beams.

LEFT Floor plan.

OPPOSITE Vertiginous 36-foot-tall (11-meter-tall) living room occupies the ground floor. The upper floor is the still soaring but more intimate setting for the master bedroom and mezzanine-level guest room.

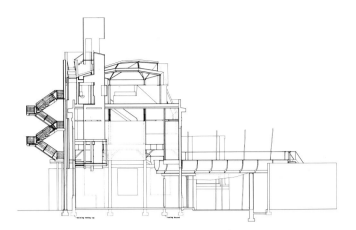

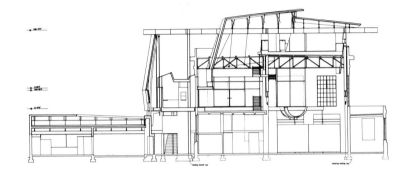

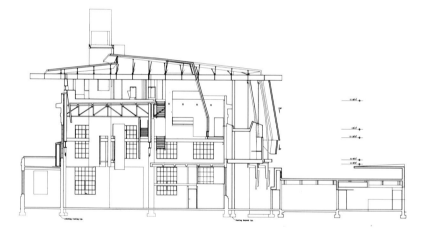

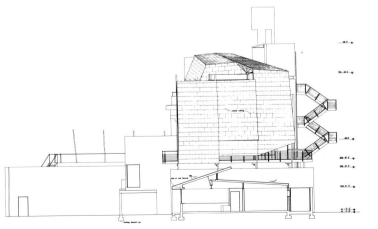

ABOVE On the ground floor is a semiprivate gallery for the owner's art collection.

LEFT Sections.

OPPOSITE Stairway leads from living area to the bedroom annex.

OPPOSITE FAR RIGHT The architects did not simply create a geometric collage of found parts. They extrapolated lines from the surrounding landscape, landmarks such as Dodger Stadium, mountain peaks, and the downtown skyline influenced the interior design.

Concrete Loft
FRANKEL + COLEMAN

THE ARCHITECTS-OWNERS of this all-concrete loft, in a landmark building in the center of Chicago's historic Printers' Row District, were interested in experimenting with living in the open. The loft's main features are concrete floors and ceilings and a series of pivoting doors, with only the two bathrooms completely enclosed. As both the owner and his wife work long hours at home, the loft is a spatial experiment designed to be modified and adjusted according to family and work needs, allowing the owners always to be in visual contact with each other. The spartan reductiveness of the interior design contributes to the wide-open feeling in this award-winning 3,500-square-foot (325.2-square-meter) loft. The owners are also fierce collectors of twentieth-century modernist furniture and art, which they rotate in and out of the loft from storage on a regular basis. The architects achieved a minimalist effect by building very few walls and installing window treatments that keep the busy city views out of sight.

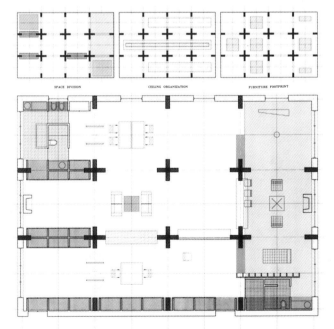

SPACE DIVISION   CEILING ORGANIZATION   FURNITURE FOOTPRINT

ABOVE Loft occupies space in a historic building in the center of Chicago.

LEFT Floor plan.

OPPOSITE The loft has been organized around twelve square bays. A central feature of this 3,500-square-foot (325.2-square-meter) space is the family room and kitchen area, which includes a built-in library and stainless-steel countertops.

LEFT Original concrete columns have been painted with textured paint to complement concrete floors and new galvanized duct work. Le Corbusier sofas and Knoll chairs (background).

OPPOSITE Long view down central axis to freestanding gas fireplace.

ABOVE The rugged kitchen features stainless-steel cabinets and commercial appliances.

OPPOSITE The working area looks through pivoting doors to the baby's quarters, which feature a custom-designed, stainless-steel crib and Alexander Calder mobile.

Coolen House
KRIS MYS ARCHITECT

THE EUROPEAN SPIN on lofts takes on a new twist within the five-story conversion of the Coolen House, a 1905 Art Nouveau villa in the city of Antwerp, Belgium. The focus was on bringing in natural light to a previously dark residence. With twenty-nine fewer doors than before its alteration, the first task of renovation was to pull out all the nonsupporting walls and open up each of the five levels to each other. To accomplish this, the architect also changed floor heights. From the top, one can look right down to the ground floor of the structure. The five-story-high central atrium also serves as a showcase for a valuable collection of fairground figures. An extension at the back of the highly ornamented building has been replaced by a rectangular box with a short wing that is cantilevered at an angle. This houses the owner's office and seems to float into the garden.

LEFT The focal point of the interior is a rust-colored steel construction with glass casing.

OPPOSITE A custom-designed steel staircase was built into the building. Floor heights were altered and walls removed.

ABOVE This loftlike residence is a showcase for a valuable collection of fairground figures.

OPPOSITE Steel and wood trusses and aluminum-backed insulation converted the dark attic into a light-filled bedroom.

Oliver's Wharf
MCDOWELL + BENEDETTI

JUST A FEW hundred meters downstream from London's Tower Bridge, the luxurious Oliver's Wharf loft development occupies a former tea warehouse. Given haute couture treatment by a rising young design team, the roof-top loft featured here offers extravagance and mimimalism under one roof in the trendy Docklands neighborhood of this capital city. The client's program was specific: Maximize the river views and create a forum for cooking, entertaining, and art while keeping the space as open as possible. The building was mostly gutted, exposing old woodwork and rustic, bare bricks. To create a metropolitan ambience, the designers mixed modern materials with original elements. Cast-iron columns were added to support oak trusses, and the walls were sandblasted. Throughout the loft, intensely colored, enameled steel screens, cabinet doors, and cast-glass slabs have been installed. The crowning feature is a rooftop terrace with 360-degree views on the Thames.

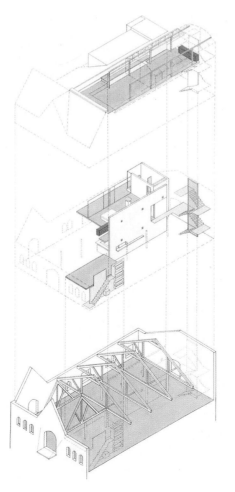

ABOVE A protected London landmark, Oliver's Wharf was built in 1870. A century later it has become one of the city's first loft-block conversions.

LEFT Exploded axonometric diagram shows how new elements were inserted into the existing structure.

OPPOSITE Spectacular rooftop pavilion offers windswept views along the Thames.

ABOVE A cast-glass stair screen illuminated from above by natural light and from below by uplights.

LEFT Enameled steel kitchen cabinets were designed to maximize light.

ABOVE The bedroom, where there appears to be nothing between the bed and the Tower Bridge but a sheet of glass.

RIGHT Two-story fireplace screen in the main living area contains not only a gas fire and bookshelves but also conceals a steel stairway.

O'Malley Residence

CARPENTER/GRODZINS ARCHITECTS

THE POLISHED 1,600-SQUARE-FOOT (148.6-square-meter) O'Malley loft is located in a small town outside Scranton, Pennsylvania. Originally a warehouse, the space was demolished to the perimeter walls, columns, and beams, leaving a virtually clean volume to accommodate the owner's very limited program request: wide-open space. The loft is intended for a single person, so privacy was a small concern and allowed the architects to keep the space open and transparent. Maximizing natural light was also a high priority for the architects. Columns, walls, and bands of marble inlaid in the oak flooring help suggest a casual order and create divisions for the living, dining, and sleeping areas. The kitchen and bathroom are placed along a window wall that faces southwest, providing ample natural light. Translucent and transparent glass built forms help define the space and circulation pattern.

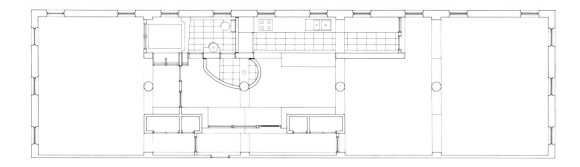

ABOVE Flanking the entry are a pair of ash- and glass-fronted storage units that suggest walls and provide closet space.

LEFT Floor plan.

OPPOSITE Etched-glass storage cabinets are featured throughout the loft.

ABOVE The main living space is dominated by columns and marble inlays in the oak flooring that break up the space. Behind the dining table, a translucent glass panel acts as a dividing wall from the entry.

OPPOSITE The bedroom is part of a seamless continuum with the main living space. The etched-glass front of a storage unit, which bridges the bedroom and entry, provides only hints of the objects within.

New River Head

MCDOWELL + BENEDETTI

ONCE THE BOARDROOM for London's Metropolitan Water Boards, this two-bedroom loft is dominated by the sweeping gestures and grand decoration of the original 1921 building. The enormous, double-height room and adjacent lobby-corridor, which features large Corinthian columns, have all been carefully restored and largely painted white. The boardroom has been turned into a huge living room with grand windows opening onto the street. The former press-corps balconies at each end of the space have been converted into library galleries reached by narrow staircases concealed behind new, freestanding screen walls that incorporate large-scale artwork. The design team introduced contemporary elements that provide functionality and contrast to the beauty of the original details. A small upper floor contains two bedrooms and a large bathroom. The new stairway leading to the bedroom floor is formed in folded, bead-blasted steel and incorporates a large fish tank as part of the landing balustrade.

ABOVE AND RIGHT Views of the main living area that was once the majestic boardroom of the London Metropolitan Water Board's head office.

ABOVE Narrow staircases leading to library balconies are concealed behind new, freestanding screen walls that incorporate large-scale artwork.

OPPOSITE ABOVE Bedroom area on the second level is serene and simple.

OPPOSITE BELOW The design team has relied on modern artwork to bring color and comedy into this largely serious loft space.

Pavonia Loft
ANDERS ASSOCIATES

A NEW WAY of living in the modern world is the motivation for the Pavonia Loft. The 5,000-square-foot (464.5-square-meter) space, in a former warehouse on the New Jersey waterfront facing Manhattan, was purchased by two families. Their housing objective was to establish an affordable residence near the city. With two families occupying the loft, novel solutions in design at a relatively low cost were necessary. Both families share the main living area, which is divided into two sections and allows for a generous common open space. Separate private spaces have been provided for each family: a kitchen, bathroom, and two bedrooms organized around a shared laundry. In character, the loft is a collision of the old and new. The use of inexpensive materials, including a fiberglass tower and subway-grate floors, is in keeping with the loft's no-nonsense industrial origins and setting.

ABOVE View of shared living area at night. Tower is illuminated from within like an enormous Japanese lantern.

LEFT Interior perspective.

OPPOSITE Main living space. Light washes through a three-story tower from a skylight above and open-grate floors commonly found in subways.

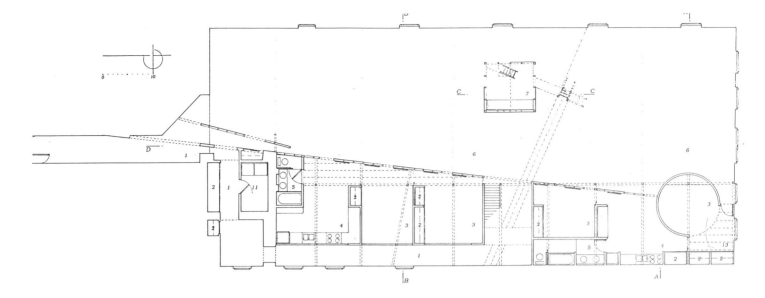

ABOVE First floor plan.

BELOW South dining room.
Orange drum is a sheetrock
cylinder with spiraling
rag-roll finish.

RIGHT South bedroom. Bridge incorporates branches of trees as ballusters. Ladder allows access to bridge from living room.

ABOVE Bridge intersection from below.

OPPOSITE Cantilevered study at night. Red desk faces tilted screen of wood and Plexiglas. Steel duct runs length of loft, approximately 100 feet (30.5 meters).

Neal's Yard
RICK MATHER ARCHITECTS

THE WAREHOUSES AND light industrial buildings of Covent Garden have long been coveted by the estate agents of London seeking fashionable digs for their clients. While certainly picturesque, the area is characterized by narrow brick buildings short on light and space. From the shell of a former warehouse building, high above the hustle and bustle of Neal's Yard, Rick Mather Architects have carved out a spectacular rooftop loft. Sunlight pours in from a central core and the space is airy and open. The client wished to be able to see the sky when he showered. The installation of laylight floor panels, including a special electronic glass that turns opaque at the flick of a switch, makes gazing at the sky possible while still allowing privacy when desired.

ABOVE Top-floor study is hidden behind a partition wall, yet is still part of the open plan.

OPPOSITE The original wedge-shaped warehouse has been cleverly manipulated by the architects. Bedroom skylight can instantly be made opaque.

RIGHT A triumph of modern style, this rooftop loft is filled with light and a collection of modern furniture.

ABOVE The central-core stair-well allows light from the zigzag line of skylights to pour down into the lower floor.

OPPOSITE Rooftop terrace provides a bit of greenery in this urban landscape dominated by chimney tops and brick buildings.

Chiswick Green Studios
PETER WADLEY ARCHITECTS

A WEEKEND PIED-À-TERRE owned by a family who have taken refuge in the suburbs, this loft is one of several in a redeveloped industrial building in West London. The 1,575-square-foot (146-square-meter), three-bedroom unit features a metallic green tower in the entranceway, which serves as a reminder to the client of the navigation buoys in the high seas that he favors. The tower serves a dual purpose as a fire wall required by London's fire code. On the reverse side of the tower is a child's bedroom with a ladder to a bed deck. The southwestern end of the loft is used as the main living area, with links to the kitchen. The master bedroom is situated at the opposite end for maximum privacy. Powder blue paint contrasts brightly with the maple floors. Cherry and stainless-steel details are featured on the doors and in the kitchen.

LEFT Powder blue paint on the built-in storage units contrasts with a metallic green tower. On the reverse side of the tower is a child's bedroom with a ladder to a bed deck; desk, sitting, and storage areas are below.

OPPOSITE In the main living area the owners chose to install minimal furnishings to highlight the beauty of built-in details.

ABOVE Built-in cherry breakfast bar features a dropped ceiling to divide kitchen from main living area.

RIGHT View along the main dividing wall that creates privacy and volume in the loft.

ABOVE View along the main access of the loft.

RIGHT Push-pull stainless-steel door handles were designed especially for this project.

Tribeca Loft
TERRELONGE DESIGN

EXPANSIVE, NEW YORK–STYLE studio loft developments, both new-from-the-ground-up buildings and commercial conversions, are the trend in many cities of Canada. In this suburban Toronto loft-block conversion, the developers called on Del Terrelonge to design a series of model suites. Custom-built details abound, including a submerged soaker bathtub. The smallest unit, at 680 square feet (63.2 square meters), offers custom built-ins and 9-foot (2.7-meter) ceilings. While many of the original elements of the building are hidden, the overall plan is clean, comfortable, inviting, and simple. Wood detailing, slate flooring, floor-to-ceiling frosted-glass doors, and a bathroom spa add to a sense of haute living. It's a far cry from the raw artist warehouses of yesteryear, as a new wave of loft dwellers seems to favor untrammeled luxury.

ABOVE Master bathroom.

OPPOSITE View of sitting area with bedroom behind frosted-glass floor-to-ceiling doors.

ABOVE View of the living area
with built-in sofa, slate floors,
and painted walls.

ABOVE Kitchen-dining area features stone tile and custom cabinetry and bookshelves.

Casa di Libri
ROSANNA MONZINI

COMMERCIAL CONVERSIONS FOR residential use are rare in Italy. The renovation of a common balcony tenement building in central Milan with lots of space but little light provided a loft-like residence for a family of three and their many books. The living room was opened at the corner and was subdivided into rooms that create interior vistas and enhance the light. The multifunctionality of a loft-like space finds definition here through the inclusion of a library around which the rest of the residence was built. The addition of iron stairs and balconies as access ways to bedrooms and bathrooms allowed the second floor to be open. Two double-height inner courtyards filled with trees and flowers create yet more vistas and infuse more light into the building.

ABOVE The library is an important part of the loft-like space.

OPPOSITE Double-height courtyards filled with trees and flowers bring light into the building.

ABOVE Entrance to the library, a *bibliothèque's* dream.

OPPOSITE The addition of balconies and iron stairways allowed the second floor to be opened for a greater flow of space.

Merchandise Mart Lofts
CECCONI SIMONE

LOFT DESIGN IN Toronto is still in a very early stage, having taken hold only in the mid-1990s. Hoping to capitalize on a worldwide trend, developers have turned to some very large, abandoned warehouse buildings for residential conversions. Purported to be the largest conversion project of its kind in North America, the challenge here was to create comfortable loft units in more than one million square feet (more than 93,000 square meters) of a former Sears building. But selling the idea of open space for domestic living is not always easy. Interior planning of the models was therefore carefully considered, with designers Anna Simone and Elaine Cecconi proposing some interesting design solutions. The loft units are mostly small and narrow, ranging from 625 to 1,200 square feet (58 to 111.5 square meters), so the designers were sensitive to the need for natural light and useful, well-defined spaciousness.

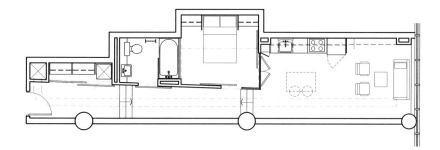

ABOVE View from kitchen area down through entrance hallway.

LEFT Typical unit floor plan

OPPOSITE An open stair in this two-level unit adds to the sense of spaciousness.

ABOVE In this, the smallest unit, high ceilings compensate for the narrow footprint.

ABOVE Stainless steel work table doubles as an eating area where space and flexibility are at a premium in this 625-square-foot (58-square-meter) loft.

RIGHT In a larger unit of the same building, frosted glass and sliding wooden panels serve a temporary function, depending on the need for privacy.

West Shinjuku

FREDERICK FISHER & PARTNERS ARCHITECTS

WEST SHINJUKU IS a contemporary loft development of thirty units in Tokyo, where space and natural
light are in high demand. Concrete and steel are the
foundation for the individual units, which vary in shape
and size. Texture, color, and warm wood were introduced by the architect for richness and to transcend a
predominantly gray environment. The plans for this
large project were streamlined to impart not only a
sense of lightness but to increase a sense of openness
in a city where space is uncommon in typical living
quarters. Narrow corridors have been abandoned.
Exposed stairs, floor-to-ceiling windows, and
mezzanines permit views throughout these double-
height loft units. Free-flowing living areas and
restrained surfaces take on a new role in this massive
and modern megalopolis.

ABOVE A concrete and steel
building provides the setting for a
large-scale loft project in Tokyo.

LEFT Typical floor plans.

OPPOSITE Residents have chosen
light furnishings to increase the
enjoyment of spaciousness.

ABOVE Mezzanines are alight with views over the city.

OPPOSITE Floor-to-ceiling windows offer natural light and a sense of space—at a high premium in Tokyo.

Bay Loft
BRAYTON & HUGHES DESIGN STUDIO

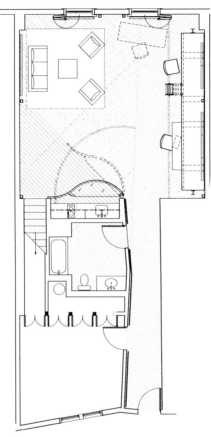

BRICKS DOMINATE THIS 1,500-square-foot (139.4-square-meter) loft for living and working in a converted nineteenth-century warehouse at the base of the San Francisco Bay Bridge. The space, uncluttered and flexible, provides an abundance of light and work space, as requested by the client. Just beyond the entrance, which is dominated by shelving for file archives, a curved maple wall on hinges and roller tracks incorporates a small glass counter for the kitchen. When open, the wall reveals the working kitchen, and when closed, it extends the corridor paneling into the main living and working area. Tall windows along the east wall look out to the bay and provide wonderful natural light. The original steel beams of the structure have been augmented with two new beams to provide a regular grid from which to hang lights. Comfortable bedrooms and bathrooms upstairs complete the loft. The architects limited their material palette to pine floors, maple casework and paneling, and milled-finish stainless steel and aluminum to bridge past and present.

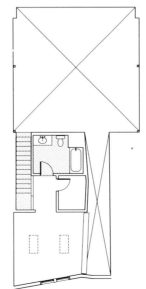

LEFT Floor plans.

OPPOSITE The choice of materials was driven by a desire to bridge the past of the former industrial space to the present. The loft features pine floors, maple casework and paneling, and milled-finish stainless-steel and aluminum.

ABOVE Six-inch (15.2-centimeter) yellow pine laid diagonally along a seam extends from the angle of the hall across the main hall. This subtle division defines the work area.

ABOVE View of the kitchen and stairs leading to upper bedrooms and bathrooms.

RIGHT View of the kitchen with the hinged maple wall open.

DIRECTORY

DESIGNERS

Alexander Gorlin Architect
137 Varick Street
New York, NY 10013
tel. 212.229.1199
fax 212.206.3590

Anders Associates
P. O. Box 2710
Midland, MI 48641
tel/fax 517.832.7030

BAK Architecture
Laura Briggs and Paola Iacucci
71 Barrow Street, No. 18
New York, NY 10014
tel/fax 212.255.9867

Belmont Freeman Architects
110 West 40th Street
New York, NY 10018
tel 212.382.3311
fax 212.730.1229

Brayton & Hughes
Design Studio
250 Sutter Street, Suite 650
San Francisco, CA 94108
tel 415.291.8100
fax 415.434.8145

Carpenter/Grodzins Architects
35 East 19th Street
New York, NY 10003
tel. 212.254.2753

Cecconi Simone
663 Queen Street East
Toronto, Ontario
M4M 1G4 Canada
tel 416.462.1445
fax 416.462.2577

Cha & Innerhofer
Architecture + Design
611 Broadway, Suite 540
New York, NY 10012
tel 212.477.6957
fax 212.353.3286

Dean/Wolf Architects
40 Hudson Street
New York, NY 10013
tel/fax 212.732.1887

Frankel + Coleman
727 South Dearborn Street
Chicago, IL 60605
tel 312.697.1620
fax 312.697.1622

Frederick Fisher & Partners
12248 Santa Monica
Boulevard
Los Angeles, CA 90025-2518
tel 310.820.6680
fax 310.820.6118

Galia Solomonoff Projects
249 West 29th Street
New York, NY 10001
tel 212.268.1569
fax 212.631.0379

Hardy Holzman Pfeiffer
Associates
902 Broadway
New York, NY 10010
tel 212.677.6030
fax 212.979.0535

Hut Sachs Studio
55 Crosby Street
New York, NY 10012
tel 212.219.1567
fax 212.219.1677

Kar Ho Architect
117 West 17th Street
New York, NY 10011
tel 212.237.3450

LOT/EK Architecture
Ada Tolla and Giuseppe
Lignano
55 Little West 12th Street
New York, NY 10014
tel. 212.255.9326

McDowell + Benedetti
62 Roseberry Avenue
London EC1R 4RR
ENGLAND
tel 171.278.8810
fax 171.278.8844

Moneo Brock Architects
145 Hudson Street
New York, NY 10013
tel 212.625.0308
fax 212.625.0309

Peter Wadley Architects
Shoreditch Studio 44-46
Scrutton Street
London EC2A 4HH
England
tel 171.377.2777
fax 171.377.5439

Rick Mather Architects
123 Camden High Street
London NW1 7JR ENGLAND
tel/fax 171.284.1727

RoTo Architects, Inc.
Michael Rotundi
and Clark Stevens
600 Moulton Avenue
Los Angeles, CA 90031
tel 323.226.1112
fax 323.226.1105

Scott Marble • Karen
Fairbanks
Architects
66 West Broadway, #600
New York, NY 10007
tel 212.233.0653
fax 212.233.0654

Terrelonge Design
477 Richmond Street West
Toronto, Ontario
MSV3G7   CANADA
tel 416.564.5342

Tod Williams, Billie Tsien and
Associates
222 Central Park South
New York, NY 10019
tel 212.582.2385
fax 212.245.1984

Tow Studios
Peter Tow
260 5th Avenue, Suite 1206
New York, NY 10001
tel 212.576.1807

Vicente Wolf Associates, Inc.
333 West 39th Street
New York, NY 10018
tel 212.465.0590
fax 212.465.0639

DIRECTORY

PHOTOGRAPHERS

Bjorg Arnarsdottir
Bjorg Photography
517 Avenue of the Americas
New York, NY 10011
tel 212.255.5258

Arcaid
The Factory
2 Acre Road
Kingston on Thames
Surrey KT2 6EF Great Britain
tel 44.181.546.4352
fax 44.181.541.5230
Dennis Gilbert
Alberto Piovano

Rico Bella
19 Lysander Court
Toronto, Ontario
MIV 3R2
tel 416.321.1364

Benny Chan
Fotoworks
824 17th Street, #5
Santa Monica, CA 90403
tel 310.449.0026
fax 310.264.9777

Billy Cunningham
140 7th Avenue
New York, NY 10011
tel 212.929.6313
fax 212.929.6318

Esto Photographics, Inc.
222 Valley Place
Mamaroneck, NY 10543
tel 914.698.4060
fax 914.698.1033
Peter Aaron
Jeff Goldberg

Hedrich Blessing
Photographers
11 West Illinois Street
Chicago, Illinois 60610
tel 312.321.1151
fax 312.321.1165
Marco Lorenzetti

Eduard Hueber
Arch Photo, Inc.
51 White Street, #5S
New York, NY 10013
tel. 212.941.9294
fax 212.941.9317

David Joseph
Snaps
523 Broadway, #5
New York, NY 10012
tel 212.226.3535
fax 212.334.9155

Chun Y. Lai Photography
119 West 23rd Street,
Studio 905
New York, NY 10011
tel. 212.645.2385
fax 212.691.1668

Norman McGrath
Photography
164 West 79th Street
New York, NY 10024
tel 212.799.6422
fax 212.799.1285

James Mitchell
62 Roseberry Avenue
London EC1R 4RR ENG-
LAND
tel 171.278.8810

Michael Moran Photography
371 Broadway, 2nd floor
New York, NY 10013
tel 212.334.4543
fax 212.334.3854

Peter Paige Associates, Inc.
269 Parkside Road
Harrington Park, NJ 07640
tel 201.767.3150
fax 201.767.9263

Tim Soar
62 Roseberry Avenue
London EC1R 4RR ENGLAND
tel 171.278.8810

John Sutton Photography
8 Main Street
Pt. San Quentin, CA 94964
tel. 415.258.8100
fax. 415.258.8167

Joy von Tiedemann
24 Tennis Crescent
Toronto, Ontario M4K IJ3
Canada
tel 416.465.0843
fax 416.465.3334

Paul Warchol
224 Centre Street, 5th Floor
New York, NY 10013
tel 212.431.3461
fax 212.274.1953

Christopher Wesnofske
Photography
280 Park Avenue South, #16C
New York, NY 10010
tel/fax 212.473.0993

PHOTOGRAPHY CREDITS

NEW YORK CITY

Urban Interface Loft, Dean/Wolf Architects, pp.14–17
Photographs by Peter Aaron/ESTO

The Ultimate Loft, Hardy Holzman Pfeiffer Associates, pp. 18–23
Photographs by Norman McGrath

34th Street Loft, LOT/EK Architecture, pp. 24–27
Photographs by Paul Warchol

Quandt Loft, Tod Williams, Billie Tsien and Associates, pp. 28–31
Photographs by Peter Paige

Family Living Loft, Scott Marble • Karen Fairbanks, Architects,
pp. 32–37
Photographs by Eduard Hueber, Arch Photo, Inc.

Tribeca Loft, Tow Studios, pp. 38–41
Photographs by Bjorg Arnarsdottir

Renaud Loft, Cha & Innerhoffer Architecture + Design,
pp. 42–45
Photographs by David Joseph

Fifth Avenue Loft, Scott Marble, Karen Fairbanks, Architects,
pp. 46–49
Photographs by Eduard Hueber, Arch Photo, Inc.

Divney Residence, Hut Sachs Studio, pp. 50–53
Photographs by Jeff Goldberg/ESTO

Hudson Loft, Alexander Gorlin Architect, pp. 54–57
Photographs by Peter Aaron/ESTO, and Billy Cunningham

Wei Loft, BAK Architecture, pp. 58–61
Photographs by Eduard Hueber, Arch Photo, Inc.

City Loft, Vicente Wolf Associates, Inc., pp. 62–65
Photographs by Vicente Wolf

Chelsea Loft, Kar Ho Architect, pp. 66–71
Photographs by Bjorg Arnarsdottir

Rosenberg Residence and Studio, Belmont Freeman Architects,
pp. 72–75
Photographs by Christopher Wesnofske

Live/Work Dualities, Dean/Wolf Architects, pp. 76–79
Photographs by Eduard Hueber, Arch Photo, Inc.

Artist's Studio, Galia Solomonoff Projects, pp. 80–83
Photographs by David Joseph

Tribeca Home and Studio, Moneo Brock Architects, pp. 84–87
Photographs by Michael Moran

GOING GLOBAL

Los Angeles
Carlson-Reges Residence, RoTo Architects, Inc., pp. 90–93
Photographs by Benny Chan, Fotoworks

Chicago
Concrete Loft, Frankel + Coleman, pp. 94–99
Photographs by Marco Lorenzetti for Hedrich Blessing

Antwerp
Coolen House, Kris Mys Architect, pp. 100–103
Photographs by Alberto Piovano for Arcaid

London
Oliverís Wharf, McDowell + Benedetti, pp. 104–109
Photographs by Tim Soar

Avoca, Pennsylvania
O'Malley Residence, Carpenter/Grodzins, Architects,
pp. 110–113
Photographs by Chun Y. Lai

London
New River Head, McDowell + Benedetti, pp. 114–117
Photographs by James Mitchell

Jersey City
Pavonia Loft, Anders Associates, pp. 118–123
Photographs by Otto Baitz and Simo Neri

London
Neal's Yard, Rick Mather Architects, pp. 124–129
Photographs by Dennis Gilbert for Arcaid

London
Chiswick Green Studios, Peter Wadley Architects, pp. 130–133
Photographs by Peter Wadley

Toronto
Tribeca Ontario, Terrelonge Design, pp. 134–137
Photographs by Rico Bella

Milan
Casa di Libri, Rosanna Monzini, pp. 138–141
Photographs by Alberto Piovano for Arcaid

Toronto
Merchandise Mart Lofts, Cecconi Simone, pp. 142–145
Photographs by Joy von Tiedemann

Tokyo
West Shinjuku, Frederick Fisher & Partners, pp. 146–149
Photographs by Motoi Niki and Frederick Fisher

San Francisco
Bay Loft, Brayton & Hughes Design Studio, pp. 150–153
Photographs by John Sutton

ABOUT THE AUTHOR

Felicia Eisenberg Molnar is a Los Angeles-based writer who specializes in architecture and design. A former editor at both the Israel Museum and the Getty Conservation Institute, she has also worked with Yale University Press, Chelsea House Press, Pacific Design Center, the Society for Architectural Historians, the United Nations Center for Human Rights, and Art Center College of Design. Her articles have been published in *Designer's West*, *Perspectives*, the *Geneva News*, and *'Scape*. Ms. Molnar lives in Topanga Canyon, California, with her husband and daughter.